SARAJEVO ROSES

POETRY FROM

A WAR ZONE

Sarajevo Roses
Poetry From a War Zone

By

Jason Markiewitz
Colonel, US Air Force

ISBN 978-0-9747259-1-8

Printed in the U.S.A

SARAJEVO ROSES. Copyright © 2025 by Jason Markiewitz. All Rights Reserved. Printed in the United States of America. No part of this book may be used or reproduced in any manner whatsoever without express written permission by the author or publisher.

This Collection is Dedicated:

To Diana

&

To all those who fought,

who risked all they had,

to defend their homes,

from dictators and tyrants.

Contents

Contents   *i*

Regional Map   *v*

Foreword by Jon Wongrey   *vii*

A Note to the Readers   *xi*

Inscription   1

Under European Moons   3

Sealed in a Crate   4

War-torn Relic   5

Sniper Alley   8

Beneath the Falling Snow   11

Lucky Ones   12

The Road to Tuzla   14

The Butcher of Bosnia   16

The NATO Van   19

Two Towns, Worlds Apart   20

The Monument   22

Turkish Coffee	23
On the Banks of the Ibar	24
Sarajevo Roses	26
Mitrovica	27
The Barbecue	30
A Hundred Marble Markers	32
Two Chimneys Standing Tall	34
Mass Grave Beneath the Snow	36
So Much for the Cat	38
No Way but Up	40
House of Usher	41
Skeletons	42
The Chill of the Air	44
A Camouflaged Captain	45
Tracks that Faced the Clouds	46
The Eternal Flame	48
Snow Fell as Fairy Dust	49
Elder Statesman	50
I'm With You Every Day	52
I Find Myself Distracted	53

Acknowledgements 55

Photographic Credits 57

Other Works by this Author 59

About the Author 61

Reviews 63

Regional Map

Foreword

> *"We are the Dead. Short days ago*
> *We lived, felt dawn, saw sunset glow,*
> *Loved and were loved, and now we lie,*
> *In Flanders fields."*

Canadian physician, Lieutenant Colonel, and poet, John McCrae's World War One poem, *"In Flanders Fields"* stands as the most recognizable and popular poem of men on the battlefield. McCrae's usage of the English language was flawless to the hairline.

Over a century has passed, many wars have been fought, and many poems written. But not since *"In Flanders Fields"* has a poem, no, a collection of poems appeared with such compassion and insight into the destructive nature of man as is found in USAF Colonel Jason Markiewitz's "Sarajevo Roses" written after serving in the former country of Yugoslavia in 2003.

When Colonel Markiewitz asked me to write a foreword for his book, *"Sarajevo Roses"* I was blindsided to say the least. Though my background is somewhat weighty in writing, war escapes me. I was on the verge of decline until after reading the first poem, *"War-torn Relic."* The sincerity of his well-chosen words coupled with his astute observation of horror and needless destruction was captivating! It was at that moment that I decided not to take an academic route, but rather that of journalistic discovery. In doing so, a bright poetic light broke through like a novel in verse.

So, I invite you to walk an enlightened path into a war so few of us know so little about.

> *"The after-effects of Civil War lingered on every street,*
> *and on the face of every passer-by who, through tired eyes,*
> *stared at me through the window; did they see a Satan or saint,*
> *with twin silver bars on a camouflage uniform cap?"*
> *- An excerpt from "War-torn Relic"*

In the poem, *"Sniper Alley"* he wrote:

> *"The assassins waited with sharpened sword,*
> *for days or more, in the deadly chambers awaiting a golden egg;*
> *a chance to fire good fortune's bullet, to kill for their reward.*
>
> *How much was life worth?*
> *A youth: $100;*
> *A pregnant woman: $500;*
> *Anyone wearing a blue helmet: $2,000."*

Those lines penned by Colonel Markiewitz pierced me to the bone marrow depicting man's coldness. An ice pick to my soul.

The collapse of mankind continued when he so deftly wrote:

> *"The rounds knew not on whom they fell,*
> *a child of ten,*
> *a mother of four,*
> *a man of the cloth.*
> *They struck without discern or desire."*

"Sarajevo Roses" is more than a great contribution of war-time poetry, it is a warning shot that man must come to the table of reconciliation.

> *"All around the city small red patches bloomed,*
> *flowering, bursting through the pavement, stretching*
> *toward eternity, yearning for tranquility and peace.*

But petals did not emerge, and this was not a garden; but rather a nameless cemetery with over two hundred resin-filled markers."

And this is where I must take my leave.

Jon Wongrey

Jon Wongrey began writing for "The State" newspaper based in Columbia, South Carolina, in 1967 and has penned over 1,800 articles and stories published in newspapers and periodicals in the US, Canada, and the United Kingdom. In 1970, he was the first writer at "The State" to receive the Conservation Communication Award presented by the National Wildlife Federation, the South Carolina Wildlife Federation, the Sears-Roebuck Foundation, and the Governor's Achievement Program for 'outstanding use of the nation's natural resources.' He is a recipient of sixteen regional and state writing awards including two awards for his book of poetry: "Moments of Glory." He is also the author of the novel, "The Last Rice Planter," a collection of short stories, "A Time Past," the novella, "The Guest," and a book of quail hunting stories, "A Covey of Tales." You can find his works on Amazon and more books are on the way!

A Note to the Readers

Thank you for reading "Sarajevo Roses." This collection of poetry and photographs was composed in large part during my time in the Balkans (former Yugoslavia) and is meant to depict the rawness of what I saw and the stories I was told while serving there. Some descriptions are graphic, and unyieldingly serve to underscore the harrowing experiences of those deployed and the people whose lives were forever changed by tyranny. Over the years, I have done some additional research on the places, cities, and monuments described in the previous pages, and discovered some inaccuracies that required correction. In an effort to be historically and technically accurate, what you read in here is meant to serve both. The photographs are only a small collection of the hundreds of landscapes, cityscapes, and architectural pictures I took, however it is my belief that the ones selected for this publication provide the best visual companion to the poetic verses.

In no way is this collection designed to support a particular narrative or provide any commentary on United States policy or involvement in the Kosovo conflict, NATO, or UN participation. The imagery, statements, feelings, descriptions, accounts, and opinions expressed in these poems and through the photographs are entirely my own and are not to be considered official statements by the U.S. Air Force, U.S. Department of Defense, or the U.S. government. I am extremely proud of my NATO brethren with whom I served as part of this Balkans expedition; some of whom were in this region years prior to 2003 and gave harrowing first-hand accounts of being present during much more intense conflict than what I certainly experienced. In particular, my hat's off to Jean-Yves, Francois, Mark, Metin, James, Philippe, Giuseppe, and my battle buddy, Guido; we all had each others' backs out there.

Since 2003, Bosnia and Herzegovina, Kosovo, North Macedonia (FYROM), Croatia, and the surrounding area has drastically changed; and for the sake of the people, I certainly hope it is for the better.

"The Lord is a refuge for the oppressed, a stronghold in times of trouble."

- Psalm 9:9

Under European Moons

Fifteen months ago, the earth stopped turning
as two New York towers fell;
a third plane hit the Pentagon,
causing damage to its shell.
A fourth plane, likely destined for
the heart of Washington
was overtaken by Patriots
before the terrorists were done.
About three thousand people died
in this synchronized attack,
by terrorists who never imagined
the Hell that we'd give back.
From that day on I've lived my life
like it was September twelfth,
and it was time I packed my bags
and deployed downrange myself.

But instead of being sent to fight
bin Laden and his goons,
my orders sent me off to NATO
under European moons.
Then off to Bosnia and Herzegovina,
before pushing to Kosovo
then forward to Macedonia
where we all were told to go.
I never knew how much of
my career this trip would hone,
from working alongside partner nations,
to serving in a combat zone.

Sealed in a Crate

Sealed in a crate, a rickety metal casket,
shoulder to shoulder with your comrade,
both showing signs of sickness as the
drafty Lithuanian cargo plane is
tossed to and fro inside the clouds.

"Heavy air currents," the pilot said,
the kind that sent your stomach
right up to your throat, then back down,
then, immediately up again.

Turbulence.
So much turbulence.
We tried to sleep. But between the shivering,
the jolting, and the jarring,
it was impossible.

You just hoped to make it in one piece,
and then not get shot when you arrived.

War-torn Relic

Sarajevo: a war-torn relic
of a world-class city;
she lay broken, a battered mother
holding a frightened child.
Gone is the beauty that once was,
when athletes took to the field
in desperate struggles to bring
back home Olympic gold.
The city that bustled with commerce
and hope on the world stage
now writhed in bullet-riddled pain;
hoping fate had not been sealed.

We drove past lonely cemeteries,
churches, and solemn homes
that, though dejected, aptly showed
the proprietors' dismay;
and snow piled high along the roads
served to hide our NATO van.
Roofs strained hard to hold the
winter's release on every structure,
and, regardless of the pain,
people still went about their lives,
as if to shake a fist at those
who just turned away and ran.

The after-effects of Civil War
lingered on every street,
and on the face of every passer-by

who, through tired eyes,
stared at me through the window;
did they see a Satan or saint,
with twin silver bars on a
camouflage uniform cap?
Artillery craters, bomb damage,
and destruction on every corner,
made keeping one's composure intact
an act of true restraint.

Photo 1: Destroyed 3-story Building/Factory in Sarajevo, 2003.
(Photo by: Jason Markiewitz)

Photo 2: Muslim Cemetery in Sarajevo, 2003.
(Photo by: Jason Markiewitz)

Sniper Alley

Our van paused briefly behind
a run-down Bosnian cab,
giving a moment for reflection
of how it used to be
a decade ago, when snipers
perched across this very road.

A poor, shoddy, two-car trolley,
rumbling on rickety tracks,
adorned in green Cyrillic graffiti,
cried out as it passed.
And like a shroud of death,
the Balkan fog lurked
and grimly strode.

On our right, a long row of
blue-white apartment buildings stood,
littered with age-old bullet holes,
like a thousand open wounds,
and broken windows told the tale
of deserted, hollow tombs.

On the left, the ravaged symbols
of freedom and hope remained;
command centers stood strong
and dared the enemy to strike,
while those at the Holiday Inn
confined themselves to their rooms.

During the war, those apartments didn't
live the life they used to have,
where families sat down for dinner,
and prayed for better days ahead,
where mothers bathed their children
and books were read at night.

That existence faded when the
snipers overtook the rooms,
and aimed their weapons out the
windows, putting crosshairs on
any on the street below, in whose
death they should take delight.

Thus, Sniper Alley became infamous;
how much is life worth?
What was humanity's value?
The assassins waited with sharpened sword,
for days or more, in the deadly chambers
awaiting a golden egg;
a chance to fire good fortune's bullet,
to kill for their reward.

How much was life worth?
    A youth: $100;
        A pregnant woman: $500;
            Anyone wearing a blue helmet: $2,000;

It mattered not who wore the symbol
of the foe atop their head,
as long as the shot was pure and true,
and as long as they were dead.

Photo 3: "Sniper Alley" Apartments in Sarajevo, 2003.
(Photo by: Jason Markiewitz)

Photo 4: The UN Mission in Bosnia-Herzegovina (UNMIBH)
Train in Sarajevo, 2003.
(Photo by: Jason Markiewitz)

Beneath the Falling Snow

I looked out of my window
on one snowy afternoon,
and watched the snowflakes glitter
painting everything in white.
I went outside to stand alone
and feel the falling flakes,
as one by one they floated by
illuminate and bright.

My arms were covered fully
as was I, head to toe,
with arms outstretched, poised statuesque,
I lay down on the lawn.
And refused to move an inch
as the snow kept falling
painting me, enveloping me,
'til I was buried alive, and gone.

Lucky Ones

They say that war is hell.
But, Civil War is worse.
And, Sarajevo felt the very worst.
Artillery shells fell as angels of death
on unsuspecting innocents.
The rounds knew not on whom they fell,
a child of ten,
a mother of four,
a man of the cloth.
They struck without discern or desire,
the unwitting participants of ethnic and political strife.
And, when they hit, those who perished
were, indeed, the lucky ones.

Photo 5: Destroyed Home Outside Sarajevo, 2003.
(Photo by: Jason Markiewitz)

Photo 6: Destroyed Home Outside Sarajevo, 2003.
(Photo by: Jason Markiewitz)

The Road to Tuzla

On a narrow winding road we drove,
the terrain, uneven, rough and rocky,
barely wide enough for us to stop;
it was covered in fresh-dropped snow and ice,
and we could feel the wheels slide and catch
as we snaked our way to the mountain's top.

Dozens of klicks from Sarajevo,
the scene was transformed before our eyes,
and the air outside was fresh and new.
Snow blanketed the hillside and the valley
below in a soft and gentle peace;
a mirage that put the landmines out of view.

Photo 7: "Snow Blanketed Hillside" Outside Sarajevo, 2003.
(Photo by: Jason Markiewitz)

The Butcher of Bosnia

What must happen to be genocide?
And how many have to die?
For the Butcher of Bosnia,
the question also should be why?

It was early May in ninety-two
and independence reigned.
But ethnic lines were not so clean,
and Bosnia was stained.

The ethnic Serbs saw no kinship
with their Muslim countrymen,
and dreamt to be united, in league,
with "Greater Serbia" again.

It wasn't long before Serbian Armies
attacked those Muslim towns
and shortly after, Sarajevo
lost her will, and lost her crown.

The Butcher drove his forces across
each hill and through the land,
while Zvornik, Foca, and Visegrad
could each no longer stand.

Mechanized strength gave courage
to the Butcher's soldiers' wrath,
who murdered, raped, and tortured
anyone who crossed their path.

Bosnians tried, with Croatian aid,
to fight and save their homes,
but by this time their country
limped away with broken bones.

And, so it was, for three years' time,
the Butcher held them down,
then in July of ninety-five,
he set to take the last three towns.

U.N. Peacekeepers never had a
chance as he rolled through,
the Butcher's armored units
overwhelmed the Dutch ones too.

Serbian forces abducted women
and girls to dirty beds,
while men and boys were stacked
in trenches, bullets in their heads.

After four long bloody months it ended,
with a U.S. brokered deal,
two hundred thousand unmarked graves
for those who would not kneel.

Whether ethnic cleansing or genocide,
the Hague just couldn't say,
But one hundred sixty-one would soon
be brought their Judgment Day.

It took some sixteen years to find him,
and the trial took more than four,
then the tribunal made its judgment clear;
guilty for crimes of war.

The clouds parted, and the sun shone down
on those who chanced to live;
the people of Srebrenica had
pushed the demons back to Hell.
And the Butcher of Bosnia,
out of appeals,
rots with devils in his cell.

The NATO Van

If blizzards were oceans
this rickety machine, laboring
down nameless thoroughfares,
passing villages as barren as
shipwrecks, navigating areas
which cartographers feigned
to care, propelling across vast
expanses of inhospitable and
treacherous terrain, where schools
of fish were swarms of bugs,
where riverbeds sank deep
toward unimaginable anonymity,
and where charting a course
through a sea of hostile white,
would be well served to have
Captain Nemo at the helm.

Two Towns, Worlds Apart

Through binoculars I saw
two towns across the field,
One was Serb and showing life,
one Bosniak in pain.

Two poor towns, worlds apart,
a lone dirt road between,
and the landmine-riddled countryside
made going there insane.

Photo 8: Damaged Serbian Enclave, Bosnia, 2003.
(Photo by: Jason Markiewitz)

The Monument

Made of marble some ten feet tall,
the monument stood reposed,
carved by hand with adoration,
it was a modern shrine;
even though less than a decade old,
it still showed signs of age,
with flowers below, covered in frost,
where mourners knelt in line.

It served as a landmark, an
ominous corner-post of stone,
and established undrawn borders,
marking ethnic party lands.
It also served as homage, to
those who fought and died in war,
in reverence to the UCK,
and their freedom-fighter bands.

The monument, one of hundreds,
each one an echoed rhyme,
uniquely built in size and shape,
like fingerprints in time.

Turkish Coffee

I admit it.
When it comes to coffee,
I'm a bit particular,
even snobbish, perhaps.
A medium to dark roast,
no cream, just black,
and please,
not the bottom of the pot.
Strong is good,
but not too much,
and burned is
as bad as weak.

But I was ill-prepared for
the unimaginable darkness,
the unbounded strength,
the unbridled fortitude,
the unfiltered density,
the unabated jolt,
and indeed, my friend,
the undeniably undrinkable sludge,
that is Turkish coffee.
I tried it.
Once.
I admit it.
When it comes to coffee,
yes, one could certainly argue,
I AM a *bit* particular.

On the Banks of the Ibar

On the banks of the Ibar,
where old buildings go to die,
the 'Confidence Zone,' as it is called,
is but an empty shell;
a desolate place with hollow walls
of businesses and homes,
designed to be cross-ethnic,
but simply ended up as Hell.

We walked down cobble streets
and gazed at empty mercantiles,
with broken windows and torn-down signs:
a vandal's Shang-ri-La;
when out of nowhere, a child darted
from behind a rusted-out sedan,
then vanished quickly around the corner
holding something in his paw.

Photo 9: The Ibar River, Looking East, 2003.
(Photo by: Jason Markiewitz)

Photo 10: Destroyed Business in the "Confidence Zone," Mitrovica, Kosovo, 2003. (Photo by: Jason Markiewitz)

Sarajevo Roses

All around the city
small red patches bloomed,
growing, flowering,
bursting through the pavement,
stretching toward eternity,
yearning for tranquility and peace.
But petals did not emerge,
and this was not a garden;
but rather a nameless cemetery
with over two hundred
resin-filled markers.
A field of Sarajevo Roses.
Each rose blossomed where a
munition crushed the Earth,
a remembrance of the travesties,
the infliction of physical and
psychological pain, a memorial
to the Siege of Sarajevo,
a bouquet for the massacred
at the hands of the purest evil.
And daily, teary passersby pollinate
these fields as if the salty
droplets would end their suffering,
stop the bloodshed,
and even bring their loved ones back;
but in the end,
only memories remain,
preserved
in the concrete.

Mitrovica

Mitrovica: a divided city;
halved by a serpent of greenish blue,
winding under the winter sun.
The Ibar River glistening,
and in the distance, one of
three gray lonely bridges,
standing proud against all odds;
bridges used more by foot than car,
and even then it's rare.

The western bridge, where people
walk from broken northern homes,
to visit family in the south,
is thin and scant and sad.
It is a change in lifestyle,
like an earthquake's aftermath,
going from south to north;
across the Ibar to and fro.
It's sad, but serves as a microcosm
 of greater Kosovo.

Cyrillic letters were painted
across North Mitrovica,
letters that served as an unspoken
guide to visitors, and travelers,
saying, "keep moving, you needn't stop,
you are in Serb territory now."
Serb territory.
Land governed from

hundreds of miles away,
as if telling locals,
"I hear you…
as long as I don't have to see you."

And in the South, two shops stood out,
in utter disrepair,
they protruded like two swollen eyes
on an alabaster face,
a twin-killing,
doors ajar,
windows broken,
the shops fight against the fates;
destruction by stones,
tossed in hatred,
from the idle hands of vandals,
with nothing else to do.

This damage was not done yesterday;
not even last week,
but rather wounds incurred
more than four years' past.
The struggling proprietors work,
to put food on the table;
to keep the lights on at home;
to give their children hope.
It's tragic, yet all too real.

And the future remains uncertain.

За Митровице.   For Mitrovica

Photo 11: The Three Towers, Mitrovica, Kosovo, 2003.
(Photo by: Jason Markiewitz)

Photo 12: Capt Jason Markiewitz with Mitrovica, Kosovo in the Background, 2003.
(Photo by: Jason Markiewitz)

The Barbecue

A strange monument.
Aptly named, we all agreed,
in form and odd design,
resembling a mix between
a rotisserie and shrine.

But it's significance
was greater than the name
we lovingly gave in jest.
The Miner's Monument,
stands proud above a city
which shall likely never rest.

It honors Albanian and
Serbian miners who lost
their lives in World War Two.
Those who fought against
the Nazis, sacrificing
all they ever knew.

Then the wars began at home.
And unity was torn apart.
And the barbecue lost its
significance; as Kosovo
lost its heart.

Photo 13: View Toward the Miner's Monument, Kosovo, 2003.
(Photo by: Jason Markiewitz)

Photo 14: The Miner's Monument, Kosovo, 2003.
(Photo by: Jason Markiewitz)

A Hundred Marble Markers

A hundred marble markers
stood sentry before the church,
with names inscribed in foreign text
both ominous and proud.

A village in the distance danced
so vibrant in the sun,
while the cemetery kneeling here
wore a melancholy shroud.

Bianca and Toma, faces
prominently displayed,
presided over headstones
with the Bakić family name.

A haunting prayer for afterlife,
when ghostly bells shall toll;
eternally wandering through the night,
where their demons did the same.

Photo 15: Serbian Cemetery, 2003.
(Photo by Jason Markiewitz)

Photo 16: Serbian Cemetery, Bakich Family Headstones, 2003.
(Photo by: Jason Markiewitz)

Two Chimneys Standing Tall

To my left, a bombed-out building,
two chimneys standing tall,
the roof was gone and weather
took its toll on all four sides.

The crumbling stone helped
snowdrifts rise along the walls,
and in the stillness, the old house
told of the death she tried to hide.

Photo 17: "The Two Chimneys" - Destroyed House Outside of Sarajevo, 2003. (Photo by: Jason Markiewitz)

Mass Grave Beneath the Snow

The wind breathed through my hair
as angels passed gently by.
My eyes clenched shut out of respect
for those who didn't want to die.

And on the air there came a sound,
a whimper, and then a hush.
A teenage boy, and then his father,
seemed to be in such a rush.

They darted 'cross the lonely trenches
on the ground where evil stood.
Do I call out? Do I ask their names?
Or do I let them go for good?

Did they see me standing there?
Did they wonder why I came?
When the child looked back into my eyes
did he wonder quite the same?

And in an instant, they disappeared,
almost as quick as they'd arrived.
Those sad and lonely apparitions
who didn't know they'd even died.

I'm not quite sure if anyone else,
had heard or seen them go.
But I know what caught my eyes today,
by that mass grave beneath the snow.

Photo 18: Damaged Muslim Enclave, Metejce, North Macedonia (FYROM), 2003. (Photo by: Jason Markiewitz)

Photo 19: National Liberation Army (NLA) Trenches, Metejce, North Macedonia (FYROM), 2003.
(Photo by: Jason Markiewitz)

So Much for the Cat

One degree Celsius.
It's not warm, but it's warmer than yesterday.
The increased temps have brought back wildlife.
A black cat walks across the snow, as incognito as a siren,
colors so vibrant against the untrammeled ice.
He sat on a three-step entry.

Two degrees Celsius.
A patch of snow fell from a nearby rooftop as
the base layer melted; a sneak attack.
He never saw it coming.
So much for the cat.

Photo 20: Camp Butmir, Sarajevo, Bosnia, 2003.
(Photo by: Jason Markiewitz)

Photo 21: Capt Markiewitz at Camp Butmir, Sarajevo, Bosnia,
2003. (Photo by: Jason Markiewitz)

No Way but Up

How many more mothers
will bury their children.
How many more wives
will bury their husbands.
How many more tears
will be used to moisten the
gardens alongside nondescript
markers in lonely cemeteries.
How many more pages will
turn on the calendar until
peace and calm prevail.
I, or rather we, as Americans,
do not live in this sort of fear.
We rise and sleep under a
blanket of freedom and
rarely, if ever, take the time
to think about places like this,
places where sleeping can only
be done with one eye open;
places where a barking dog may be
followed by a detonated mine;
places where corruption and
strife are words even the young
will all too fully comprehend.
Shania's voice danced in my ears
while my eyes looked upon the chaos.
At that moment, her lyrics were poignant,
and I couldn't agree more;
"...there's no way but **up** from here."

House of Usher

A not-so-insignificant crack
ran latitudinally from the ethnically
and architecturally symbolic roof.
A pyramid of tile above a perfect
square structure, which from the
outside could have been drawn
by any child with fingerpaints,
butcher paper, and imagination.
Asymmetrical window frames once
housed glass and a barren entry
barred visitors despite the missing door.
It looked ill, and if it had not fully
lost the battle against this mysterious
ailment, its time was definitely near.

While many parallels existed in this
dubious and ghastly House of Usher,
no siblings ran from within and no
melodies from some ghostly guitar
lurking among the bricks could be heard.
No paintings could be viewed from
without, and while the sky was overcast,
it did not seem that this place would glow.
As if finally succumbing as we drove away,
it faded slowly into the evening mist,
and I watched,
while it sank,
into the horizon.

Skeletons

The aftereffects of the war are everywhere.
Bullet holes decorate homes,
artillery impacts on apartment buildings,
and craters sat juxtaposed them all.

As far as the eye could see
skeletons of houses where families dined,
where evening prayers were said,
and where children played,
protrude through the snow as a
grisly reminder.

The attack was here in the kitchen,
the battlefield was out in the yard,
and the family was left dead in the ashes.

Photo 22: Destroyed Houses in Matejce, North Macedonia (FYROM), 2003.
(Photo by: Jason Markiewitz)

Photo 23: Destroyed Makedonian Complex, North Macedonia (FYROM), 2003.
(Photo by: Jason Markiewitz)

The Chill of the Air

The chill of the air,
the nip of the night,
the old man moves
by candlelight.
Winding through trees,
and guarding the moon,
as distant gray wolves
howl outlawed tunes.
The wind plays her flute,
the sun's down 'til dawn,
and through the
mist and the cold,
he moves on.

A Camouflaged Captain

At times I feel like a journalist,
describing what I see
with camera and pen,
describing in detail,
finding the right words
to evoke the affect
I wish to convey.
I also feel like a voyeur,
drawing back the blinds,
peering into the lives
of unacquainted souls,
exposing the nudity,
the bare imagery on
unashamed display.

Perhaps an archaeologist,
excavating remnants,
building a reference,
exploring the unknown,
gently unearthing the keys
to a painful puzzle
before my eyes.
Indeed, I am all these, and more,
a camouflaged Captain,
traversing the war zone,
capturing the details,
and the imagery,
and the remnants,
and the lies.

Tracks that Faced the Clouds

It was a sight I had never seen before.
Seventy-two thousand pounds of metal,
a machine of war; the rumble of which
sent fear into the hearts of the locals;
the cannon fire of which concussed the air;
the firepower of which was enough to
tear buildings apart with a single round;
the metallic screeching of wheels braking,
axis turns, as its turret fixed on target;
the imperviousness of which eradicated
hope as it thundered through the streets.

But the people rallied, and fought, and died,
to resist the onslaught, to push back
against the genocide, to stand against
tyranny, and give each breath for freedom.
And the result of their resistance could not
be more visual than the sight of a seventy-two
thousand pound main battle tank, no longer
striking fear, but rather reminding all of their
victory, lying dead in the snow, upended,
with tracks that faced the clouds.

Photo 24: Serbian T-54/55 Tank in Matejce, North Macedonia (FYROM); left as a symbol of victory. This tank was the exact one that attacked the Mosque pictured below. 2003.
(Photo by Jason Markiewitz)

Photo 25: Mosque in Matejce, North Macedonia (FYROM); with holes left from tank attack. 2003.
(Photo by: Jason Markiewitz)

The Eternal Flame

Travelling through Bosnia,
a fractured country at best,
with Serbs and Muslims juxtaposed,
where SFOR strains to keep the peace,
our unit traverses past the bridge where
the Archduke Ferdinand was killed.

The bridge now stands as a landmark,
reconstructed in part, preserved through time,
it spans a small river that creeps through the city;
a lonely waterway, whose silence is haunting,
where the smallest babble, no matter how faint,
can be heard for miles around.

As one passes through the destruction,
the indiscriminate ruin and rubble,
signs of life sprout; with progress on the rise.
A small shrine glows in the dreary distance,
with a fire easy to recognize,
surrounded by patrons and mourners alike.

It burns continuously, a symbol to
the people that better days are ahead;
to remind them of what used to be.
The people say it stands for prosperity,
for liberation, for the homeland.

The Eternal Flame burns,
and the people have faith.

Snow Fell as Fairy Dust

I was struck by the silence,
the eerie stillness
in the early dawn,
my breath acting
as the sole source of life
at this moment.
A literary scene made
by Medusa's gaze.

Snow fell as fairy dust,
sparkling, smiling,
calling out to me
with the volume
of a mime.

Elder Statesman

Deep ruts line a weary face,
though not produced from laughs.
A month or more his beard has grown,
unkempt and mostly white.
Graying eyes, sharp and focused,
with no tears prepared to shed,
recounting all this soldier saw,
squinting in the morning's light.

The elder statesman watches us,
and no words are said aloud.
A cigarette hangs from a crooked mouth,
as he sits straight, and tall, and proud.

Photo 26: A View into Skopje, North Macedonia (FYROM), 2003.
(Photo by: Jason Markiewitz)

Photo 27: Downtown Skopje, North Macedonia (FYROM), 2003.
(Photo by: Jason Markiewitz)

I'm With You Every Day

The stars came out tonight.
In truth, they've been out before,
but I hardly noticed.
I have no idea what constellation
is above me right now,
and I am uncertain if
you can see it too.
But, if you can, know this.
Know that I love you.

Know that I love you
more today than yesterday.
Know that my heart is warm
despite the weather, as this
gold band on my finger says
I'm yours and you're mine.
Know that while I'm across the world,
I'm with you every day.
And I know that you're with me too.

I Find Myself Distracted

I find myself distracted, deep in thought,
not of anything that would change the world,
but of the world outside this barracks;
that which I have seen, what I have witnessed,
what I have been told, and what I felt.

And in the darkness that colors the landscape,
both by time of night and happenstance,
my thoughts are of home, my family,
my country, not ripped apart by war,
or crushed by the thumb of socialism.

We yearn for what we do not have,
while these people here need that which
we do not fully appreciate; and while some
at home wish to keep up with the Joneses,
no one here cares, as it doesn't help them eat.

Acknowledgements

I would be remiss if I didn't acknowledge the numerous people who have had a positive impact on my writing over the years. This includes teachers, mentors, family, and friends, and every member of the United States Armed Forces, past and present, who have sacrificed so much to ensure that this country remains the shining beacon on the hill, and a place where liberty and freedom will continue to be defended until our dying breaths.

I also want to acknowledge Jewel Kilcher, yes, that Jewel, who is not only an amazing musician but is also a tremendous poet. I read her book *"A Knight Without Armor"* upon its publication in 1998 and was so taken by the imagery she created in each verse, I began to refine the dozens of poems I had written over the past 7-8 years and submit them to various anthologies. After winning a Second Place prize from River Road Press in April 2001, and having two other poems accepted for larger anthologies, I began to believe my writing may actually be worthy of publication. Between that newfound confidence, and the inspiration from Jewel's book, I took the plunge to publish *"Beneath the Mojave Desert Moon"* in 2003.

I graciously acknowledge my poetry colleagues Veronica Jarboe, author of *"Sweethearts and Sorrows"* and *"Dragon Girl,"* A.A. Rubin, author of *"Into That Darkness Peering"* and *"The Awful Alphabet,"* and others who have positively influenced my poetry and my life.

Additionally, I gratefully acknowledge Jon Wongrey, the prolific writer, photographer, chef, entrepreneur, and poet, whose award-winning writing career has spanned more than 50 years with over 1,800 articles published across the U.S., Canada, and England in newspapers, magazines, journals, and cookbooks. I am grateful that he took me up on my request to compose a foreword for this book and I greatly value his friendship.

Finally, I am humbled to acknowledge the unwavering love and support my wife, Diana, has given me over our more than two decades of marriage. She has spent plenty of time alone with remote assignments, deployments, and even short-term exercises or temporary duty assignments. Through it all, it has not been easy, and thanks to her, we survived it. I owe her more than she will ever know, and all who have served, or are currently serving, know well that the member in uniform is not the only one who sacrifices during our tenure in the military. She has been a squadron key spouse, a detachment key spouse, and will always be the key spouse in our family. Thank you, sweetheart. I love you more than you can possibly imagine and look forward to all that the coming years have to offer.

Photographic Credits

All photos contained in this book are provided from the extensive photographic collection of Jason Markiewitz. During his forward deployment to Kosovo, Bosnia and Herzegovina, and the Former Yugoslav Republic of Macedonia (FYROM) or North Macedonia, he took more than 300 photos depicting the damage those places suffered during the preceding decade of conflict. All photos are the property of Jason Markiewitz.

Cover Art photo of an actual Sarajevo Rose is in the public domain and can be found here:
https://commons.wikimedia.org/wiki/File:SarajevoRose.jpg

Other Works by this Author

Books:

"Beneath the Mojave Desert Moon" (2003)

www.markiewitzaudioworks.com/books

Audio Dramas:

"The Raven"

"The Cask of Amontillado"

"Manuscript Found in a Bottle"

"The Tell-Tale Heart"

"Three Christmas Trees"

"A Visit From St. Nicholas"

"Artaban and the Quest for the King"

"A Cratchit Christmas"

www.markiewitzaudioworks.com/audio-dramas

Audiobooks:

Dozens of books narrated by Jason Markiewitz can be found on Audible.com or wherever you get your audiobooks.

About the Author

Jason Markiewitz is the author of the previously released collection of poetry entitled, *"Beneath the Mojave Desert Moon"* (2003, *Morris Publishing*). He was awarded a second-place finish in the April 2001 *Poet Voices* National Competition for his poem "Meet Me in the Valley" and his works have been featured in four international anthologies.

When not writing, he serves as an officer in the United States Air Force, having been stationed in Italy, Korea, Afghanistan, and the United States. He was forward deployed to the Balkans (former Yugoslavia region) in 2003 which inspired the works comprising "Sarajevo Roses."

In addition, he is an award-winning audiobook narrator and audio dramatist, with more than 35 titles currently available on Audible, having worked for some of the best authors in the business including USA Today and New York Times Bestselling Author Lorhainne Eckhart and USA Today Bestselling Author Liz Isaacson. He is a recipient of four audiobook narration awards and four audio drama award nominations including a 2023 Saturday Visiter Award Finalist Nomination at the International Edgar Allan Poe Festival and Awards in Baltimore, Maryland.

He resides in California with his wife, Diana, their three children, and a Labradoodle.

Reviews

"Every now and then, we are fortunate enough to witness art that is strong by its weakness, beautiful in its ugliness, and sweet through its bitterness. The poetry within these pages is crushingly lovely, even though its subject is often bleak. In Sarajevo Roses: Poetry from a War Zone, Markiewitz does not shy away from the difficult things, but rather stands facing them... and because of that courage, we can face them also. This is the true purpose of art--to frame life's best and worst, allowing us to grapple with nightmare and what, for some, becomes reality."

- Craig A. Hart, Author
  Baxter Kids Adventure Series
  Maxwell Barnes Adventures
  Shelby Alexander Thrillers

"The poem that haunts me is 'Sarajevo Roses;' in the middle [of the book], yet the most poignant. I just can't let that mental picture go. I can identify with this collection, flying so many nights over the Bosnian, Serbian, Kosovoan skies."

- Leslie Maher
  Brig General, USAF (Ret)

"Gritty. Raw. Genuine. Born of war and delivered from the soul, Sarajevo Roses is a timeless collection of war-inspired poetry that will resonate with the heart. Sarajevo Roses is a visceral experience for the senses that will leave its readers spellbound.

The truth of war and its devastating effects are unmasked in this expertly penned poetry collection. Angst filled, I turned the pages as Jason Markiewitz took me behind enemy lines, painting a picture in my head with his riveting words and photographs that will stay with me. This collection is a haunting memorial to those who came before us and a warning to those who will inherit the future we build."

- Holly Knightley, Author
  Knight Time Novellas

"The rich garden of images and words full of raw emotion that is Sarajevo Roses invites readers to experience it in a visceral manner. Accompanied by intricate images, readers get a glimpse into Markiewitz' stunning collection of poetry. One glorious poem fluidly feeds into the next and upon the last page, the realization that it went too quickly, sinks in. That is what Sarajevo Roses is, it is an experience like no other collection of poems has done before. A journey of real life instances blended with beautiful words, has a way of pulling readers in and not letting them go. Experience Sarajevo Roses and what Markiewitz has uniquely crafted in its pages. The rawness and humanity in each poem, opens up the conversation of what it truly means to live and be human. Absolutely stunning!"

- Veronica Jarboe, Poet/Author
  "Sweethearts & Sorrows"

"Sarajevo Roses by Jason Markiewitz provides a biographical reading tour through a war tormented land told from a real-life point of view with his living history in verse. Markiewitz delivers a soulful, vulnerable history of his time in Kosovo and Bosnia. His poems are anchored with figurative language beaming from each page with personification - "those apartments didn't live the life they used to have"; with simile - "Artillery shells fell as angels of death on unsuspecting innocents"; and with many allusions to mythical places such as Shang-ri-La and mythical beings such as Medusa. However, his strongest use of figurative language is imagery with an example such as "snowflakes glitter" to reel you into the poem as if you are a mere traveler on the road as he shares his tales. In addition to his poetry, he adds several photos he took while stationed in Kosovo and Bosnia, which truly intertwined his words with his pictures, giving the reader the full picture of the remnants of war. The old proverb from Italian or French origin, "Every rose has its thorns," comes to mind with this collection in that all places have beauty like the rose, but the fighting brings the thorns of war and devastation. Markiewitz delivers an impactful poetic champion in Sarajevo Roses–a must read!"

- Carmen Bouldin, Teacher
Host, 6 Degrees of E.A. Poe

www.ingramcontent.com/pod-product-compliance
Lightning Source LLC
Chambersburg PA
CBHW051956290426
44110CB00015B/2267